Channels of Mercy

A true story
of one woman's victory
over pain

Bev Bodge Webster

Copyright @ Paradigm Graphics 2019

All rights reserved. No part of this book may be reproduced in any form or by any means without written permission from the publisher.

ISBN # 978-0-9653232-1-5

Published in the United States of America by
    Paradigm Graphics
    7 Hilltop Drive, Burlington
    MA 01803, 617-933-9893

Distribution and customer service: www.channelsofmercy.com

Dedication

My Mother's incurable cancer in early 1992 was a storm in our lives. I praise you, Lord, for keeping Mom with you as she battled cancer and for giving her courage and will, and for using me to minister your word for her comfort.

The shock of cancer turned from pain to joy with her hope and faith in Jesus. I thank Him that we shared the mysteries and miracles through the power of the blood, through the power of the Holy Spirit, through the power of His word, and through the power of prayer.

The Lord is our rock; we stand firm on your promises. Even though we walk through the valley, we fear no evil, for you are truly with us. I prayed for wisdom, Lord, and understanding; that my words would be your words, that my ministering hands would be yours.

I dedicate this book, which you directed me to write for you and through you, to my Mom. My precious Mother, I love you ...This is for you.

This is for you too, Bill Watt, used as a vessel of the Lord. You told me that my writings should be in a book. I love you friend.

My 21 month old son Jay went to be with the Lord in 1961.

Mom went to be with the Lord on Nov. 22, 1992, and Bill Watt also went to be with the Lord on Feb. 22, 1996.

My daughter Janine went to be with the Lord on Sept. 11, 2010. We miss you "Neenie."

Precious in the sight of the Lord is the death of His saints.

This book is also dedicated to my remaining children, John, Jill, Jamey, Jo-Ellyn and Jim; and all my grandchildren whom God gave me to love.

Acknowledgements

Thank you Lord for preparing the way for this book.

Veera Mogilicherla, Paradigm Graphics – *Thank you for all your help; design work, printing and prayers.*

Tom – *Thanks for your love and help.*

My family – *Thanks for your love.*

Marguerite – *Thanks for your long distance prayers and love.*

Dr. Charles Stanley – *Thanks for your Godly teachings.*

Pastor Roger Cousineau, East Auburn Baptist Church – *Thanks for your Christian love, counseling and support.*

Our church family and Pastors at Lisbon Falls Baptist Church – *Thank you for your Godly teachings and prayers.*

Contents

Introduction	The Journey	5
Part One	Childhood and Children	9
Part Two	Injury, Pain and Triumph	16
Part Three	Channels of Mercy	30
Part Four	Channels of Blessings- Aware of His will	36
Part Five	Channels of Light	46
Part Six	Epilogue	59

The Journey

This book is about a journey - - a journey with my Lord Jesus Christ, my savior. As a child, I felt comfortable and secure in a church atmosphere. I'll tell you about that later.

This journey has been made with my hand firmly in the hand of Jesus. But, even with a background of a childhood that was joyous not only in a religious setting, it was not always thus.

Do you recall the advice on how to get across a point to a recalcitrant listener? First, you hit 'em on the head with a 2x4, and, having attracted their attention, you can explain your point.

Well, that's what happened to me. I believed I was a good enough person and that I was living a Christian life. I was almost satisfied.

Apparently, God wasn't, because one morning at work, I was struck on the head so severely that I was in constant pain and unable to work.

My energy, used up in enduring the pain failed early in the day. There was no position that was comfortable for me at night.

The pain was my constant companion but, through the miracles of my Lord Jesus – I was healed.

This book is about Him - - and me - - and the miracle of my healing - - and your healing, if you'll let it happen.

Bev Bodge Webster

May I Touch You

May I touch you,
as Jesus has touched me?
The pain is real,
but the beautiful day I see.
He just made it for you,
He just made it for me,
to open our eyes
to all that He gives.
Through my pain and His,
companions we live.

This man so pure
died on the cross;
took on your sin and mine
so that we might live forever
the abundant life with Him.
May I always live with faith,
take time to think of others.
In place of my pain,
may I think of yours?

Saved by the Power

For my determined purpose was to know Him,
this man who died for me.
To be like Him, for He is love.
Filled with your grace, Jesus, I thank thee.
You laid the foundation for me; you are my rock.
As I glory in you, Lord, I thank thee for your
wisdom, righteousness and sanctification.
Thank you, Jesus, for your calling.
The light you've given to my life,
and for my life, brand new.
I shall tell the world how I love you.
May I always be kind to the Normans of the world.
The ones who have nothing. May I share what I have.
The different look about them.
May they see my love as I give them a meal,
a shirt, or a ride to church.
The glory is yours, Lord, as you shine through me,
for all to see that Jesus loves all - -
particularly the Normans of the world.

Part One

CHILDHOOD

AND

CHILDREN

The Beginning of You and Me

You planted the seed inside my mother's womb
and it became me.
This little girl inside of me remembers how it was.
Thank you for making me a little girl - -
a little girl to love.

You loved me then, as you do now.
I thank you, Father,
For making me your vessel.
This gift you gave me as you set the plan for my life.

I loved my mother and dad,
there were just we three.
I prayed for a baby sister or brother,
but you said no to me.
You knew I was lonely as I prayed.

But then, you gave me the 23rd Psalm.
As I recited it to myself,
I knew you were there,
the Holy Spirit in my heart. So young - - maybe nine.

The peace in my heart was coming from you.,
and the richness of your love.
The loneliness would go away: You filled my soul.
"The Lord is my shepherd, I shall not want."
A smile would appear on my face.
I felt good and warm inside.
I felt so special and loved
that I recited it often. People would ask,
"Why are you smiling?"
I really couldn't answer them; I really didn't know.
Jesus was in my heart, but I didn't know it then.
Now I do, for you have brought me close to you.

You've led me to your pasture, to be with you,
and it has restored my soul.
I sought the paths of righteousness and you guided me.
I feared no evil, for I knew I was never alone.
My cup does run over with your love
and is running over with your grace.

You gave me the privilege of
having seven beautiful, healthy babies.
Two of them, Jay and Janine, are with you now.
The remaining two daughters and three sons are
now adults, and of whom I love so much.
Each has grown to be
a caring, productive, loving adult.

Thank you, Lord, for the mom and dad I had
and for the good times.
My step-dad; the grandfathers my children knew;
they were all loved.
And maybe that's all it takes - - Forgiveness is in my vocabulary.
All parents make mistakes.
Please forgive me for the ones I've made.
We do the best we know how.

Thank you, Father, for revealing to me, a child,
That I would someday be special.
I hung on to that promise.
For your faithfulness, your promises true,
for bringing me through the valley of the shadows,
oh, Lord, how I praise thee,
For the heartaches, suffering, pain,
I praise thee.

When I turned to you, you blessed me with a gift - -
a gift of writing, to tell the world
"See, He's chosen me, special."
And, inside still, a little child,
listening to the Father.

Thank you, Lord

Thank you, Lord for blessing me with
John, Jay, Jill, Jamey, Janine, JoEllyn and Jim.
You answered that prayer of a little girl who
prayed for someone to love and care for, to share with.
That little girl, so long ago,
didin't really understand your power.
But she's in me still and she understands now.

Thank you for this wonderful family
you gave me to love.
That's all I had to give, Lord - - Love.
But you showed me that's all it takes.

Mom

The years have gone by so quickly, but the Lord has
provided time for us
to get together again in His joy and our love.
I am handicapped, but
I thank God for all these blessings,
for what I can do; especially for you.

Glory to God for saving you, baptizing too,
and leading you to following Jesus Christ.
Through my injury,
and you 60 years young,
it happened.

Praise God for He gets all the glory.
I love you, Mom. Thanks for worshiping with me.

Exodus 20:12
*Honor thy mother, that the days may be long upon the
Land, which the Lord thy God giveth thee.*

Good Morning, Lord.

Isaiah 50:4
*Morning by morning He awakens me and
opens my understanding to His will.*

My burdens I give you, Lord, for you
want peace for me.
In my heart, deep inside, as it glows,
knowing you care, you provide my needs.
This perfect day you are here with me.

Spring is coming!
I see new little birds feeding on your provisions
and feeding on the sunshine you spread forth.
You warm our day. You warm our hearts.
Your love warms us with all the blessings you bestow.

The Well-Rooted Tree

Jeremiah 17:7-8
Blessed is the man that trusteth in the Lord...for he shall be as a Tree planted by the waters and that spreadeth out her roots.

Deep, well-watered roots, luxuriant,
firmly rooted in the Word of Christ.

Spending time with our Lord and Savior,
We will have trust and faith only in Him.
We will bear the good fruit of a well-rooted tree.
Fellowship with Christ as He is...
our wisdom, our guide, our life.
He gives us the choice - -
free, to be like the well-rooted tree.

Christlike, I choose to be.

Higher for you

Father, may I go higher for you?
Friend, go higher up, you say.
Thank you Jesus for your grace,
For you have brought me to a higher place.
Obedient to you, ministering your word,
It's all I know or want to know.
Out of love, with you in my heart,
Is the only way I want to live.
Without you, Jesus, I am nothing
And surely I would die.
Please help me to be obedient to your word,
To hear your call, no matter what or where.
I only want to go higher for you,
My friend.

Faith

Dear Heavenly Father,
This world tries to squeeze me.
The disagreeable are with me.
They are everywhere.
I'm just passing through.
This is only my temporary home, my testing ground.

I believe in you, Lord.
I believe you can do anything.
My faith has matured throughout my life.

My obedience has been such a joy.
I obey you to please you,
to put into action your plan for my life.
The only way I can live is to walk in the spirit.

Take me by the hand. Lead the way.
Tell me who needs a visit,
who needs a card,
what to say and when to hold my tongue.
I listen to the Holy Spirit from my head to my heart.

Part Two

INJURY

PAIN

TRIUMPH

Will This Suffering Last Forever?

I am in chronic pain and could be for the rest of my life. The diagnosis is disc and joint disease due to the trauma caused by the injury.

The pain radiates - - neck, arms, spinal column, throughout my body - - and is always there. As I tire, it intensifies. There can be no relief in surgery, since the risk of paralysis is too great; relief through pain suppressants also suppresses my awareness, so I can't use them.

We are to give thanks for all things - - so I give thanks to God even for all the suffering and pain. All things do indeed work together for the good for those who love God and who are called according to His purpose.

He called me to minister His word and to tell my story to the world. Since I can do all things through Christ who strengthens me, and through his mysterious interventions, there have been many, many happy times for me as I worked toward obeying His urgings to get his book written and published.

Scripture says that God oversees our life, working every circumstance, if we let Him, to bring us to Christ. I've tried to be obedient, and this is the result - - Here is my story. I pray it will bring joy and strength to you as you travel the path to God.

The Accident

I was seeking the Lord and His will for me.
My children were grown, my life my own.
My son and his wife invited me to church with them.
There, I received Christ into my heart,
attended regularly, but didn't yet have
a truly personal relationship with my Lord.
I wanted to know Him better, but I didn't know how,
didn't know what He expected of me.
But He knew.
So, on a beautiful morning in April, 1988,
the Lord grabbed me as I said "Good morning"
to my coworkers as we all entered work.
I didn't know what hit me.
WHAM!!!

Was it a door? A two by four? Or was it more?
It was a heavy steel door, falling on my head and neck.
A severe whiplash injury...
no little knock on the noggin.

Yes, Lord, you got my attention right away.
I asked, as we all ask: "Why me, Lord?"
After many doctors,
more pain than I ever thought I could bear,
I turned over my life to Him.
I finally accepted that
He could work good from this, too.
His will not mine.
I would do whatever the Lord would have me do with my life.

After about a year of just praying for others,
I asked my Lord and Savior if he would heal me.
As I prayed, I felt my body experiencing
a force that lifted me up.
It didn't heal me or even alleviate my pain,
but I took it as a promise that
He would heal me one day in his perfect timing.

Right away, he began working.
He opened a door for a bible study.
He opened a door for a personal relationship with Him.
He opened a door of a vast room
filled with spiritual food
for a hungry, thirsty, frightened and lost soul.
He was - - and still is - - with me everywhere.

I've become a prayer-and-praise woman.
I find joy in helping others, visiting the sick,
writing a note of comfort which He dictates.
I'm called to write this book
which the Lord is blessing to His glory.

Pain

Dear Heavenly Father
As I awaken, I thank you for this day.
It is dreary and raining outside,
but I will rejoice in you,
and maybe sing a hymn or two.
I will try to enjoy the day.

The pain is so intense,
But I shall continue to write to you.
Thank you for your grace.
It's sufficient for me.
It's so hard at times, Father.
I only make it as you take me by the hand.

Father, I love you, and thank you for
your word and wisdom to me.

I yield my life to Jesus, I yield myself to you.
I thank you for my life,
for taking the burdens off my heart.
The peace I feel is you.

Father, I know the nearness of you
I feel you close, the miracle of the Master's hand.
My merciful Father, I count my blessings, one by one.

You always know my heart, my feelings of despair.
Giving way to my grief is hurtful,
for my holy interest has touched others, too.
So the duty is mine to press on.

The Christian Courage

Long ago, I had a friend with an artificial leg. I admired her for her courage as she went on with her life, never complaining.

Because of her handicap, I just couldn't understand her cheerful attitude.

Now I do - - she was, and is, a Christian.

I often think of her, especially during the early days following my accident. Now I know where her joy comes from.

The Doors Opened

I turned my life over to God,
It was a miracle, you know.
He saved my life.
Then, I came to know Jesus Christ
who died on the cross for me, a sinner.

It was tough for a while
not being able to work, struggling to recover.
Then the Lord took over, as it was His will all along.

Be patient, Child,
someday the divine plan will all come together.
Patience. The hardest fruit for me to bear.
But the Holy Spirit guides me every day,
by the grace of God's love.

2 Corinthians 12:10 B
For, when I am weak, then I am strong.

I think of you, Lucille, and your handicap,
and how it must have been for you.
But God loves you,
and His grace is sufficient for you, as it is for me.
God never closes one door without opening another.

Take Up Your Cross

Take up your cross and follow me.
The power of spirit through prayer will be.

Take up your cross and follow me,
Channels of mercy you will be,
bear my fruit on the branch.

Jude 1:21
*Keep yourselves in the love of God,
looking for the mercy of our Lord Jesus Christ unto eternal life.*

Take up your cross and follow me.
Channels of blessings I'll make for thee.
See the Kingdom on earth.

Take up your cross and follow me.
Channels of light I'll shine on thee.
Carry my yoke with joy.

I'm still thirsty. I'm still hungry
My day begins with Him and ends with Him.
I work for Him.
I praise Him for my life brand new
and thank Him for the blessings too
What a privilege to be constantly aware of His presence.

I take up my cross daily and we walk together.
His grace is sufficient for me; I could do nothing alone.
May the fruit of His grace show on my face,
a witness for others to see and share.

Touch My Pain

In constant pain, I walk by faith,
Christ indwelling in me.
Christ walking with me.
Yes, you are there, in me.
The power I feel is you.
The power of the Spirit coming through.
Constantly aware of your presence,
the touch of your hand on my pain, the mysterious God.
I thank thee, Lord.

Peace and Prayer

Father, Creator of this day,
the sun shines through the windows of my bedroom.
May I use this day to glorify you in any way I can.
This pain is here. Yet, I am filled, too, with your grace.
I'll endure.

I can bear it only through you, Lord, and I know it.
I've prayed without ceasing.
I've been in your word
and I pray for your wisdom. The glory I give to you.
In all things I give thanks, including the pain.
I do have a peace, Father.
I realize the shower comes before the sunshine.
You continue to show me.
So, peace, you say;
Be still and know me.

Psalm46:10
Be still and know that I am God.

Blessed By Thy Name

Blessed by thy name, Jesus.
Nobody ever loved me as thee.
As I walked through the valley of death,
He was with me.

As He walks with me daily,
As He lives within,
Blessed by thy name, Jesus.
Keep me from sin.

Thank you, Lord, as you take my hand
and guide me through the rough days.

Push on I must and you show me the way.

I know I'm doing right
as the Holy Spirit tells it to me,
and I know my heavenly Father will never forsake me,
through my best friend, Christ Jesus.

Hebrews 13:5
And be content with such things as ye have for He hath said,
"I will never leave thee, nor forsake thee."

Why Me, Lord?

As Suddenly, as God crushed me.
He brought joy to my life.

God's perfect plan for me,
to experience what I have inside - - Grace.

I treasure His power, victory as I experience it
victory over pain.
To glorify you, Lord.

The necessity of crushing me ..
just as I was seeking His will in my life,
He grabbed me.

I reached for the Master's hand
and He found mine.
As my faith deepened, my life completely changed.

Lord, obedient I will always be
The love in me is You, the power of your grace.
Blessings of your power, unending, I see.

Thank you, Lord, for your grace and strength.
My supply of life
one day at a time.
Your promise of an abundant life, Lord,
I never knew 'til now.

The Test is the Same as 2000 Years Ago
1 Peter 1:9
Receiving the end of your faith, even the salvation of your souls.
Go through a crisis in character.
Take time to pray and ask him
to take your day for His glory.
In hardship, take time to look to Him.
Give Him the burdens, and a peaceful heart will appear.
Take time to smell the roses, to look around.
God's touch on us is profound.
Walk with God and He'll make the burden light.
Seek Him first, His will to know.
The Kingdom will be yours.

Glory and Pain
In severe pain, I awoke this morning
with you on my mind, Jesus.
My heart is full of you --thank you.
My cup runneth over,
for you have given me a thankful heart
with the Holy Spirit flowing out.
I pray you will keep me full.
My suffering I bear, for your grace is sufficient for me.
You have revealed your work for me - -
to pass on the good news.
I have become a vessel for you,
for you gave me a life so indescribably beautiful...
content to be whatever and where you want me.
I shall make the most of me --so happy with life now,
brand new, brand new in you, with a peace in my heart
and a joy as you guide my hand.
The glory is yours.

Philippians 4: 11
For I have learned in whatsoever state I am
therewith to be content

We Are Vessels

Thank you, heavenly Father, for using Jerry as a vessel
for me today.
Your message did not go void, as I heard every word.
In Ecclesiastes I heard you say in everything you do,
you have a purpose and everything is in your timing.
There is a time for healing, a time to break down
and a time to build up.
You built me up today, as I recommitted my life to you.
You spoke and I heard every word.
My works, Lord, I do for you and for you I want to do.
Bless my brother Jerry, for he is my brother in Christ - -
a Godly man is he, and you have called him to go all the way.
He announced today, in faith, that you will bless him
with a license to preach your word.
For your glory, and your will, Lord. We are your vessels.
Ecclesiastes 3: 11
To everything there is a season and a time for every purpose.

Priscilla

I love you, my first Christian friend.
We worked together when we met, almost instantly
Why we crossed paths was evident.
Christian sister, somehow we already knew in our hearts.
We attended Sunday school and in church
sang praises to the one we both love, our Lord Jesus.
The day we went to the ocean - - how beautiful the trees,
remember? I shared with you my place of solitude.
Only God could do all this - -the world is so beautiful.
You understood me and I, you. Our honesty, our rare
friendship,
a very special love we shared, dependable and true.
I'll always be there for you.
Just as He will always be there for us.

The Cross

I suffer daily, Lord, in chronic pain, as many do.
Lord, I love you for suffering for me.
You died on the cross and cried out,
"It is finished."
Thank you Jesus
for being obedient to the Father unto death.
For the good God, our creator,
will give us and does give us a joy never known.
With you in my heart, Jesus,
my Lord and my Savior,
Nailed to a tree, you died for me
marked as you were, obediant to death on the cross.
As you live at the right hand of the Father,
may I be of good fruit, obedient too.
I know you have a place for me.
I want to look into your face
and see your beautiful soul.

Job 13:15
Though He slay me, yet will I trust in Him.
2 Timothy 1:12
For I know whom I have believed
John 14:2
I go to prepare a place for you
John 19:30
Jesus said It is finished.
Philippians 2:8
*He humbled Himself even to death
on the cross.*

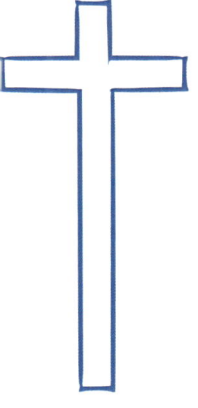

Thorns

Awesome Father that you are,
All things work for good.
Even in chronic pain, I thank you,
In all things we are to give thanks.
This is understood.

For you loved me first,
and watched me as a child.
Your hand always on me, I feel it even now.
So, I thank you, Father,
for your love, undefiled.

The love you give, incredible.
The pain is so intense.
Through my pain, I glory in the Lord
and ask: Keep me constantly aware
of your constant presence.

Minister my word, you said.
This I try to do.
And I think of Paul
with the thorn in his side.
I have my thorn, too.

I ask, Father, for your will, not mine, but thine. Living with pain, even with pain, through you, I have just begun to live.

The blessings from you, large and small - - thank you for them and for your Son, for knowing Him, the greatest blessing of all.

Part Three

CHANNELS

OF

MERCY

My Prayer

Romans 8:34
*It is Christ who is at the right hand of God,
who also maketh intercessions for us.*

I am in the direct line
of the intercession of our Lord and of the Holy Spirit.
Strengthened by His love,
which is the cure for my weary heart.
The strength that brought Him victory
brings me victory over pain.
I shall endure it
through His strength and His grace.
Thank you, God, for what you've made me,
molded me into the likeness of you.
I love you unconditionally,
and know you are taking care of me.
Thank you, Lord, for interceding in my life.
Amen and Amen.

Merciful God

James 5:11
Behold we count them happy which endure.
That the Lord is very pitiful and of tender mercy.

I praise you, God, for the merciful God that you are.
I cry unto you, my soul is yours.
Humbly I bow down in prayer,
for I know you hear the song in my heart and soul.
I love singing praises to you.
May you glory in my new life, whatever I say or do.
Minister my word, you said.
My obedience to the Lord will never end,
for your blessing to me is the abundant life.

The Tip of My Tongue

The Lord, oh, how He's blessing me, for now I'm writing
poetry. Tanja, I look forward to seeing you ...
my prayer partner you used to be and, oh, how I miss you.
Helping me to grow as a Christian ...
How grateful I am for the seeds you planted along the way.
Out of obedience to the Lord, you worked with me,
to see my feet planted solidly.
Now Jesus is my rock, as He is yours.
A fisher of men is what you are,
as I hope to be, in obedience to the Lord.
Now I am blessed everyday by Jesus Christ,
who is always on the tip of my tongue.

A Prayer for Morning

Father, I praise you, as I see the sun rising,
another beautiful day you have made for the world to see.
May we see and know the power of you.
May we be glad and rejoice in it.

As I dedicate my day to you, to your glory,
You take me by the hand once again.
Father, I know that without your presence
I will not know the way.

I know you will never forsake me.
I know you will answer every prayer
in your perfect timing.
I love you, my Father and in Jesus' name I pray.

And for the Night

Oh, Father, thank you for guiding me through the day ....
and now, through the night.
My heavenly Father, just hold me tight.
Even though I know you love me,
even though I know the power of the Holy Spirit,
a little lonely human place remains.
It all goes back to the cross and the resurrection.
it all goes back to Jesus Christ.
The hope, love, power of you, my awesome, wonderful God.
Romans 8:18
I shall consider the sufferings of the present
not worthy to be compared to the glory of the future.
How I love you for revealing to me
my place in your plan. I glory in you, forever.

Grow Up

Proverbs 2: 10
*When wisdom entereth into thine heart
and knowledge is pleasant unto thy soul.*

Grow up spiritually, don't always be a babe.
The good things you'll miss if you don't grow to full age.

Christians need to grow through the power of prayer,
reading his word.
The abundant life you' ll know here on earth.

Thank you for taking my burdens, Lord, from day to day.
The peace in my heart, knowing you have control
and the plan in your hand.

The power of you, as you bless me;
the burden you lift from my heart.
I pray for your will to be done
and the power of prayer, I know!

You Are There

You are there when I retire in the night.
You are there in the morn.
You are there when I need to talk.
You are there when I need a friend.
You are there, for you first loved me.
You are there, dear God, as I walk.
You are there when I need a hug.
You are always there for me.
I can't live without my Lord,
Unconditional love.

For This Day

Father, I thank you for this day, for the peace inside I feel.
The day is beautiful.
As you guide me through, I feel beautiful, too.
In pain again, yet I still have things to do.
I never would make it without your hand.
My heavenly Father, God above, God of love,
Thank you for filling me.

With a smile on my face, I lie here thinking of you.
Even in pain, I'm in touch with you.
I feel joy just thinking how it will be
when I get to look at thee if I dare.

I thank you, Father, for the blessing of Tanja's call.
When you answer prayer, what a blessing to know
you hear and care.
You give me the desires of my heart,
big or small, in your perfect timing.

I praise you, Lord, for your loving kindness and your mercy. My prayer to you at the start of this day: Please help me. Keep my heart clean and free from iniquity.

Part Four

CHANNELS

OF

BLESSINGS

...AWARE OF HIS WILL

We Are as One

Without you, Jesus, I can do nothing.
Without you, I cannot live.
Without you, my prayers will not be answered.
Without you, I have no grace.
Without you, I would be lost.
Without you, my heart would lose its gift of love.
Thank you, Jesus, for being the vine,
for choosing me as one of your branches.
For you, may I bring forth good fruit.
May I love and forgive as you have done for me.

John 15:5
*I am the vine, ye are the branches. He who abideth in me
and I in him, the same bringeth forth much fruit.
For without me, ye can do nothing.*

Use Me

Use me, Father, to tell your truth,
Your wisdom and guidance I seek for my life.
All I achieve is through the power of your Holy Spirit.

I ask for your guidance in pouring out to others,
ministering to them,
as you called on me to do ... this is my duty,
to work for you.

The wheat will grow right beside the tares.
As we seek God's will and serve Him through the church,
He will take care of the weeds.
We are waiting for the harvest - -
the return of Jesus Christ.

Love our enemies until the harvest comes.
Learn to turn the other cheek until the harvest comes.
Do God's will until the harvest comes.
Be kind until the harvest comes.
Be forgiving until the harvest comes.

Follow His will, and be not moved.

In pain, Father, I accept it and shall be content.
For you have said: I will never leave thee.
I grab this promise from you.
I need this promise to live.
I cry, feeling my pain and His pain
as He died, nailed to the cross, for me.
If pain is the rest of my life, I accept,
for you will reveal all to me.
You will renew me, keep me in touch,
teaching me to know you, to be like you ...
from your heart to mine.

Alone

I lie here, alone with you, Lord, in the sadness of the night.
The sound of rain outside my window,
dripping softly to the earth.

I love you so, Lord. Without you I would die.
The rain is peaceful, your whispers, saying I'm never alone,
for your Grace fills my soul.

I pray, Lord, that someday in your plan, you choose for me
a Godly man who loves you as I,
and someone to share your plan.
Praying together!
I can't imagine the ecstasy of loving you,
and each other.

Lord, in your perfect timing, I know it will be
another answer to prayer for me.
Alonetime with you is something I need,
but sharing my life and you with another!
I will patiently wait on thee.

The Long Way Back

My almighty God, I love you.
I love you with all my heart.
As sisters and brothers in Christ,
we just love one another as you first loved us.
And forgive we must, to resolve any hurt, as you forgave us.
I love them all
and, Father, you know my heart.
With a prayer in my heart, and a song just for you,
your hand led me today
to pray for a sister's forgiveness.
She must deal with you in prayer over her heart,
just as I had to, over mine.
In prayer all week,
you showed me
the long way back to your house of worship.

Spring

Spring is here, and the rain comes pouring down
to cleanse the earth and to beautify.
You made this wonderful, wet day I see.
The flowers will sprout up from the gardens,
our lawns will become green again instead of brown.
Trees will be budding and beautiful too.

Everything needed a cleansing.
I pray, my Father, that you will cleanse me
as I begin my day with you.
Thank you, Father, for the Holy Spirit,
the peace and joy in my heart.
Thank you for being in control of me ....
I feel so good inside.
Thank you for answering prayers.

Victory Over Pain, Through Jesus Christ

Dear Heavenly Father,
you get all the glory for the gift you've given me.
For the gift of love through Jesus Christ
to write this book for thee.
To tell the world how hard it is to be handicapped ...
there are many, just like me.
The impact on one's life and the whole family.

Even so, Lord, how richly you've blest me.
My broken dream I'll never have;
Go to the top, my dream, so that I could take care of me.
My restrictions now prohibit that dream,
but your promise is always true:
You never close one door without opening another.
This, you have done for me.

You brought me through the valley and gave me life,
a reason to live.
In despair, I turned, and you loved me
and gave your only begotten Son for a wretch like me.
I take up my cross and follow you, Jesus,
as I walk in my life brand new.

I'm proud to be a Christian and I will always be,
for the greatest reward is heaven and life eternally.
My faith in my God is as a rock,
He hears my every cry and he hears my every praise.
The power of prayer,
the power of the spirit works today in me.

Power of Prayer

Thank you, Bill, a blessing to me and a vessel of the Lord.
You planted the seeds; how they have grown
from a small blessing to a large, wonderful tree.
A tree of life, for the Lord has shown me my purpose for living.
Minister my word, He always said to me.
A miracle of the Lord when you planted the seed of a book in me.
"Pray," you said, and pray I did, fervently.
In His word, He revealed the truth to me.
A book He wanted, to minister about my life, my life
brand-new, even in pain, through Jesus Christ,
my Lord and Savior.

Thank you, Father, for Bill and Lois
and the Christian Bookstore.

Bill Watt so inspired me with his Christlike
nature and wisdom.

The bookstore was an answer to prayer for me.
I frequented it and they became dear to me.
I miss you Bill.

Linda - - The Beauty of a Rose

Linda, you accepted me, believed
in me, supported me.
Depressed, I walked into your
office that first day,
as I was falling apart.

The injury took my dream away - -
The dream of a career and going to
the top.

Perseverance in hand, taking
courses,
trying with all my might,
something always held me back.

Where was I now? What was I meant to be? Why me?

These past two years, so difficult.
I don't believe I could have done it without you.

With the many doctors I've had to see,
lawyers, appointments, the deposition you had to do - -
I appreciate you. All the extra stresses.
You helped me through.

Through your prayers & attires;
you were always there with me.
Yes, you and God.
Thank you, Linda, for always listening,
your encouragement, your support.

God never makes mistakes.
He sent me to you because
He knows you are the most helpful,
caring, loving, person in your field.

My Dearest Friend

Dearest Marguerite,
I miss you so. I pray for our paths to cross again,
if only for a little prayer to the One we both love.
And Dan, too; I pray for you,
as the Lord uses you to His glory.
God's blessings are bestowed upon you in Spain,
as you both teach "One-on-One."
And on me for how close we've become.

Marguerite, it still comes to mind,
shortly after I became a brand new babe:
"Pray for 'One-on-One' "you said,
I didn't know what I was praying for,
but I knew that it was good.
So, I was obedient to your request.
Then, one day, the question arose - -
where shall we hold "One-on-One?"
A tugging at my heart said: "Here it shall be" - -
thus, the Lord spoke to me.

Thank you, Marguerite, for leading,
and teaching His wisdom.
I was seeking to know Jesus Christ,
and the Father already knew what I needed.
Another miracle of answered prayer - -
"One-on-One" was here.

When Eyes are Opened

The trees are beautiful today, Father,
with snow clinging to their limbs of brown.
The beauty, Father!
Thank you for the white blanketed ground,
as slippery as it is.

I appreciate this day that you have made,
that I can see the beauty of you in nature;
and that, today, I am able to get out and drive, too.
The little things mean so much;
You don't realize, until you become out of touch,
just getting outdoors is sometimes impossible for me.
Thank you, Jesus, for opening my eyes,
for showing me your goodness, love and joy.

A Sinner

I reached for the Master's hand - - and He found mine.
He showed me what was inside,
a Holy Spirit I never knew.
Jesus was there all the time.
Through the Holy Spirit, the power of you,
the love we share,
no love could compare with anything at all.
Thank you for my life, brand new,
the one you gave to me, I now give back to you.
Yes, Jesus, I love you, a mirror I would be
To do for others, as you've done for one - -
a sinner - - me.

Part Five

CHANNELS

OF

LIGHT

Psalm 5:3
My voice Thou shalt hear in the Morning,
Oh, Lord, in the morning will I direct my prayer
unto thee and will look up.

Awakening Joy

The pleasure of my morn is awakening
with you on my mind.
Father, I thank you for this beautiful day,
the sun you have made.
Thank you, Father,
for bringing all this into my life.

In my hurt, my pain, I enjoy the beauties of your hand.
The sunrise, sunset, your warmth for the earth.
As I live one day at a time, Father,
please take me by the hand once again
and show me the way.

As I sing to you, with Jesus in my heart,
may I glorify you in everything I do.
Thank you, Father, for Jesus.
This is my prayer to you ... the first one of the day.

All Things Working Together

Romans 8:28
And we know that all things work together for good to those who love God, to those who are called to His purpose.

I press on in faith, Father,
as you've called me to do - - a blessed calling from you.
In your patience I must stay,
as you fill me with your grace.

You provide all my needs to make this calling fruitful.
I thank you.

The turmoil all around, the daily problems of the world,
Jesus, keep my eyes on you instead.
The powers I see, your miracles, Lord,
in what I do and say.
The peace, as you bring me back to life,
not leaky, but whole, I would be.
I praise thee, I praise thee, Lord.
Please keep Satan away.

Psalm 95:4-5

In His hand are the deep places of the earth;
the heights of the hills are His also.
The sea is His for He made it; and His hands formed the dry land.

My Ocean, My Lord

A fear of the ocean. Respect I have. The fierceness
of the waves.
A warning of your fierceness?
A fear of you, Lord, and I shall obey.
I praise thee for loving me enough to discipline me.
As always, my almighty King, you have my praise
for hallowed is thy name.
thy will be done on earth as in heaven,
for I take for myself, with love, your promises.
I praise thee for what you are about to do,
for what you have done.
I love to share this place, Lord,
this place you brought me to, by the sea.
I love to share this gift with others,
about how you changed my life,
from darkness into light, Lord,
with your unconditional love.
Here, in this special place of beauty,
I hear the rumbling of your power,
the whisper of your power
as you speak to me.
The tide is coming in.
I hear and see your love.
I enjoy your blessings every day.
Your presence is as incredible as the peace you give.
I look at the sky so blue and know that, for now,
paradise is right here.

God is Love

Flowers
grow in the darkness so mysteriously.
The Master's hand plants the seeds
and we can't see them grow ....
until one day ...

Flowers
so beautiful, from the fruit of the spirit,
there they are ...
the power of you, Lord ...
how I love thee ....

Love
and joy, peace, long-suffering, gentleness ...
Thank you, Lord.

So rich we are who bear your fruit,
the greatest of these being love.
Anything given without love is nothing.
Love is of God - - God is Love.

The Enemy

Satan, the enemy, alive is he.
He has a plan for you and me ... wants us to confess certain things,
to be of bad fruit, so he can party.

Satan's arrogance: I will be like the most high, says he.
We can be brought down to hell, even as Satan fell.

Satan had freedom of choice. Iniquity was found in him.
Sin. Unworthy thoughts.
Cut down to the ground was he, the devil.
Thrown down from heaven by God most high.

Paradise is with God. Come home with Jesus.
Many will live from the tree of life.
Heartaches and sorrows are of Satan.
Man willfully chooses to go against the light.

Where there is trouble, there is Satan.
He loves to break up homes,
come between family members.
Thanks be unto you, Jesus, who give us the victory.
Do away with all weeds in the garden,
plant new seeds and watch them grow.

So, when I feel Satan trying to interfere,
I say: "Flee, in the name of my Lord and Savior."
My faith is in Jesus Christ, the one who died for me.

Call on Me

Psalm 118:24
This is the day the Lord hath made;
We will rejoice and be glad in it.

O, Lord, I just love to do anything you call me to.
I enjoy being obedient to you,
as this is my purpose for living.
A praise-and-prayer warrior for you.
Sending a card, singing to your glory, visiting the sick,
you lead the way.
Thank you, Lord, for blessing me so abundantly.
I can never repay.
I love you for my life brand new.
You gave your life for me.
So, any little thing I can do to your glory, you can call on me.

My Father

Lord, the day is rainy and bleak outside.
Just knowing you made the day brings it a purpose.
The feeling of warmth inside,
the closeness I feel with you, Lord,
I thank you.
I thank you for making me, too, Lord,
for making me as you did.
The heart you gave me, filled with love.
The miracles I see all around me are from you.
Thank you for being my awesome, wonderful Father.
Just knowing you made me gives me a purpose.

Precious Water

Precious to me is my love, the ocean.
The beauty of the Lord's creation I've seen.
With winter just ending, we've forgotten the warmth.
The ocean, still so cold, yet beautiful
The water so blue, the love I see and feel all around.
The presence of you, Lord.
The peace there for me,
my daily retreat with you.
I see it again, with spring in the air.
Your favorite color must be blue - - -
your ocean, your sky - - -
you made blue your speciality .

First Day of Spring

Thank you, Father, another beautiful day.
The sun shines through, warming the house.
The sunset so beautiful, too;
your special touch, peeking through the trees.

Then, in prayer with you,
the only way to begin each day,
will you, I ask, will you take me by the hand;
take me, lead me?
For your will is what I want to do.
Oh, God, my awesome God, I ask, I ask of you
just keep me full.
Full of the Holy Spirit as I live my day,
the only way, full of you.

The awesome power of the Holy Spirit.
Lord, I ask, in prayer,
please forgive me of all my sins,
aware and unaware as I am.
Christ, take control, to overflowing.
Just keep me full. Full of you.

Let me not worry, be lonely, or need for anything.
I give you control. I know you'll provide.
You're always there.
Yes, Jesus, it's the first day of spring;
what a blessing, another blessing,
yet another blessing, my Lord.

I Glory in the Lord

Job 22:29
*When they cast you down, and you say,'Exaltation will come!'
Then He will save the humble person.*

John 15: 16
*"You did not choose Me, but I chose you and appointed you that
you should go and bear fruit, and that your fruit should remain,
that whatever you ask the Father in My name He may give you.*

I glory in the Lord, though the heartaches are many.
I glory in the Lord, though there are trials I've been through.
I glory in the Lord, though there are difficulties daily.

Only with my hand in His have I made it.

I glory in the Lord for his holy calling.
I glory in the Lord for giving me life brand new
to bring glory to Him.
Thank you, Lord, for choosing me special
to do your holy work
to minister what you have done for me
and for so many blessings,
I must count them on the beautiful tree of life.
Lord, may you bless my book,
as I glory in you, for your glory.

My Friend

My dearest friend is Jesus; on Him I can depend.
When I'm alone, I'm not, you see.
I have Him to love and to hold.
He understands my heart, my prayers,
as I humble myself for Him.
Yes, Jesus is my closest friend,
and my love, so dear, to the end.

John 3:29
"He who has the bride is the bridegroom;
but the friend of the bridegroom,
who stands and hears him, rejoices greatly
because of the bridegroom's voice.
Therefore this joy of mine is fulfilled.

Psalm 139:23-24
Search me, O God, and know my heart:
try me, and know my thoughts:
And see if there be any wicked way in me,
and lead me in the way everlasting.

I Can't Wait, Lord

Father, I send thanks and praise
for the awesome, wonderful God that you are.
I just praise you, Jesus, for finding me.

Thank you, Jesus, that I can rebuke Satan
when I feel him around me
because of your power,
the power of the Holy Spirit in me.

In the book of Mark - -
how miserable that ordinary man was
because he was full of supernatural demons.
And then you came, Jesus and set him free.
You sought him out and gave him a peace in his heart
he had never known before.

Yesterday, pastor asked the big one - -
Are you ready to go with Jesus,
if He should come right now and ask:
Why Should I Take You to My Heaven?

Father, I thank you for Jesus.
I thank you, Jesus, that you've saved me.
And - - yes, I'm ready.
I can't wait to see you.

The Book

Thank you, Father, for your grace and righteousness.
If I sin,
I claim it,
and forget it.
Please help me to stay full.

Thank you, Father, for the grace of your love.
happiness is created in me
and I learned to love me
as you first loved me
and still do.

You've called me to write this book.
You made it all possible
through the power of the Holy Spirit
and prayer.

Yes, you convicted,
provided
and guided.
I pray this book - - yours and mine, Lord,
is a blessing to everyone who reads it.

EPILOGUE

Hebrews 11: 1
*Faith is the substance of things hoped for,
the evidence of things not seen.*

Adversity Purified My Faith

Adversity strikes each and everyone of us at some time in our lives. Maybe through losing a loved one, through divorce, physical pain, mental pain etc. But we have choices. We can choose to accept it and deal with it and go on in faith or we can give up.

I pray you are comforted knowing there is hope.

The Turning Point in My Life

After mom's death, now grief stricken and still in chronic pain, I was in despair after numerous doctors, numerous medications that made me ill, therapists that really hurt me and it was now five years since the injury. The Lord had promised to heal me years ago, and since He hadn't, I thought He must have changed His mind. I really wanted to be with Him so I asked Him to take me home. Apparently His answer was no, because He sent my daughter Jo-Ellyn to fulfill His promise to heal me. Jo-Ellyn rang the doorbell many times until I had to get out of bed and answer the door. She threw me into the shower and made me promise to see one more doctor. Reluctantly, I did agree and went to see that Doctor.

The Healing

He prescribed pool therapy (exercising in a swimming pool) three days a week. I decided to give it a try. At first it was very difficult, but after several weeks and much to my surprise, I started to see improvement. The therapy was building muscle in my back and alleviating the pain. It took about one more year before the pain was completely gone and I was truly healed. I continue to go to pool therapy to keep my muscles strong.

Thank you Jesus for healing me through pool therapy. I thank you Lord and praise you with all my heart and soul. For your promises true, how I love you. You are such a faithful God.

I have written this book through the power of the Holy Spirit. I was no writer. During the five years I was in pain, He would awaken me in the night and dictate what to write. I kept all of these writings and one day shared them with Bill Watt, a Christian book store owner. He urged me to write this book. Who, me? The Lord used me as His partner. He blessed me with this spiritual gift for His sake, His glory.

These adversities, the pain and suffering, have turned to tears of joy and thanksgiving.

Now, I am so blessed with the opportunity to help others achieve their goals, their dreams. I dream of serving You, Lord, in a mighty way.

I can't even comprehend the blessings and the miracles that the future holds.

**I pray that you, the reader,
will choose to turn your adversity from pain to joy.**

ORDER FORM

Please send _____ copies of Channels of Mercy @ $12.95

                                         Subtotal for books $_____

S & H -- $3.95 first book, $0.75 each additional book

Priority shipping -- $8.35 first book $_____

                                                Sub Total $_____

                                            5.5 % Sales Tax $_____

                                                       TOTAL $_____

Send personal check payable to: Leslie J. Press
                                                           P.O. Box 223
                                                          Brunswick, ME 04011
                                                          lesliejpress@gmail.com
                                                          www.channelsofmercy.com

Ship to Name: _____

Address: _____

City, State, Zip: _____

Include gift card from _____